GIVE BEES

A CHANCE

SWEAT Bee

(COLLECTS SALT FROM HUMAN & ANIMAL SWEAT!)

SQUASH Bee

(BUILDS UNDERGROUND NESTS!)

SOUTHEASTERN BLUEBERRY Bee

(HOLDS ON TO FLOWERS AND VIBRATES WINGS TO SHAKE OUT POLLEN!)

MINING Bee

(DIGS TUNNELS IN THE EARTH!)

WOOL CARDER BEE

(COLLECTS FUZZY FIBERS FROM PLANTS TO LINE ITS NEST!)

EUROPEAN HONEYBEE

(WORLD'S MOST COMMON HONEYBEE!)

CELLOPHANE BEE

(LINES UNDERGROUND NEST WITH A SECRETION THAT DRIES TO LOOK LIKE CELLOPHANE!)

COMMON BUMBLEBEE

(IS A MASTER OF TOMATO POLLINATION!)

GIVe Bees
A CHANCe

WORDS & PICTURES by bethany bARTon

bzzz?

PUFFIN BOOKS

SURE YOU DO!

DIDN'T I TELL YOU THERE ARE ABOUT 25,000 DIFFERENT KINDS OF BEES TO LOVE?

EUROPEAN HONEYBEE

LEAF-CUTTER BEE

SQUASH BEE

EASTERN CARPENTER BEE

MINING BEE

SOUTHEASTERN BLUEBERRY BEE

AND THEN I TOLD YOU ALL ABOUT the THREE TYPES OF HONEYBEES!

QUEENS

LARGE, FERTILE FEMALE
JOB: MAKE ALL OF THE BABY BEES

JUST 1 PER HIVE

300-500 PER HIVE

DRONES

LARGE MALES
WITH NO STINGER
JOB: FIND A QUEEN TO MATE WITH

AND WORKERS

SMALL, STERILE FEMALES
WITH STINGERS
JOB: EVERYTHING ELSE!
GATHER NECTAR, POLLEN, & WATER, MAKE HONEY, FEED BABY BEES (LARVAE), BUILD & PROTECT THE HIVE, MAKE ROYAL JELLY TO FEED THE QUEEN... AND MORE!!

30,000-80,000 PER HIVE

Mostly because of their "stingers, and attached venom sacs, which are the cause of painful bee stings."

...that part you told me last week.

BUT THAT WAS JUST ONE BEE!

COULDN'T YOU STILL GIVE BEES A CHANCE?

MAYBE I JUST NEED TO REMIND YOU HOW WEIRD AND COOL A HONEYBEE'S ANATOMY IS?

FIVE EYES

- 3 TINY SIMPLE (ONE LENS) EYES, CALLED OCELLI
- 2 LARGE COMPOUND EYES WITH THOUSANDS OF LENSES!

TWO STOMACHS

- HONEY STOMACH, OR "CROP", FOR TURNING NECTAR INTO HONEY!
- BEE STOMACH, FOR DIGESTING NECTAR

BEE-PERATIO

MAyBe You Just NeeD SOMe TIMe to Get to KNOW THeM? HOW ABOUt MILLIONS OF YEARS!

YOU KNOW, Bees LiVeD WitH DINOSAURS.

SCIENTISTS HAVe FOUND Bee FOSSILS FROM MILLIONS OF YEARS AGO!

AND EVEN ANCIENT EGYPTIANS Kept Bees.

HieROGLYPHIC SYMBOL FOR Bee

PERFECT! MAYBE YOU JUST NEED SOME HONEY! BEES MAKE HONEY!

Why are you telling me all this stuff?

SO YOU'LL GIVE BEES A CHANCE!

check out How Honey is made!

A Bee GATHERS NECTAR FROM FLOWERS

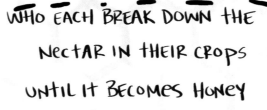

NECTAR Goes into A SPECIAL HONEY STOMACH CALLED A "CROP"

X-RAY VISION

WHO EACH BREAK DOWN THE NECTAR IN THEIR CROPS UNTIL IT BECOMES HONEY

THEN THE HONEY GETS BARFED INTO A HONEYCOMB CELL

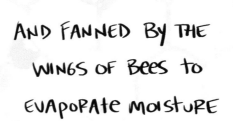

AND FANNED BY THE WINGS OF BEES to EVAPORATE MOISTURE

CONTENTS OF THE CROP ARE SPIT UP INTO A NEW BEE'S MOUTH

THE NEW BEE BREAKS DOWN THE SUGARS OF THE NECTAR WITHIN HER OWN CROP

THIS PROCESSED NECTAR IS PASSED ALONG TO SEVERAL MORE BEES

LASTLY, IT'S SEALED WITH BEESWAX TO KEEP IT SAFE (UNTIL IT'S EATEN)

...did you say barf?

JUST ONE POUND OF HONEY TAKES TWO MILLION FLOWERS AND THOUSANDS OF BEES to CREATE...

IT LOOKS LIKE I HAVEN'T CONVINCED YOU JUST YET...

Nope! Because they're all gonna sting me!

OH. WELL, BEES <u>DO</u> STING <u>SOMETIMES</u>... BUT NOT BECAUSE THEY'RE MEAN!

STINGER STORIES

Bees ONLY STING to DEFEND THEMSELVES

YOU LOOK DELICIOUS!

BACK OFF!

OR to AVOID GETTING SQUISHED

OR SMASHED

IN FACT, MANY BEES LOSE THEIR STINGER AFTER ATTACKING

WHICH IS SORT of LIKE YOUR HAND DISAPPEARING IF YOU PINCH YOUR SISTER!

You know, I love honey... but I'd be willing to give it up forever to never see a bee again.

BUT GIVING UP BEES MEANS GIVING UP SO MUCH MORE THAN JUST HONEY!

SOME SCIENTISTS SAY BEES ARE RESPONSIBLE FOR A THIRD OF ALL THE FRUITS AND VEGETABLES WE EAT!

BEES HAVE A BIG IMPACT ON THE FOOD CHAIN.

YOU SEE, IN ORDER FOR PLANTS TO GROW FRUITS AND VEGETABLES, THEY NEED the RIGHT INGREDIENTS.

SUN

WATER

POLLEN

A MAJOR INGREDIENT THEY NEED IS POLLEN.

BUT SINCE FLOWERS CAN'T MOVE, THEY CAN'T ALWAYS GET POLLEN FROM EACH OTHER.

I WANT to MAKE A STRAWBERRY... THROW ME SOME POLLEN!

I DON'T HAVE ARMS.

THAT'S WHERE BEES FLY IN...

A BEE'S FUZZY BODY CATCHES POLLEN FROM FLOWERS.

POLLEN FALLS INTO THE NEXT FLOWER THE BEE VISITS.

THEY ACT AS A POLLEN DELIVERY SERVICE, HELPING GIVE FLOWERS THE INGREDIENTS THEY NEED.

A SINGLE BEE CAN VISIT OVER 1,000 FLOWERS A DAY, MAKING BEE POLLINATION POWERS UNPARALLELED!

WHICH MEANS WITHOUT BEES, THERE'D BE A LOT LESS YUMMY STUFF to EAT.

AND BEES ARE DISAPPEARING IN LARGE NUMBERS.

BEES ACTUALLY NEED OUR HELP.

MISSING

NAME : Bee
OCCUPATION : POLLINATOR

POSSIBLE REASONS FOR DISAPPEARANCE :

PESTICIDES

PARASITES CALLED VARROA MITES

LACK OF BEE-FRIENDLY FLOWERS

POLLUTION

HONEY

Won't that just attract MORE bees?

HOPEFULLY, yes!

BUT JUST APPROACH A BEE LIKE YOU WOULD A DOG YOU DON'T KNOW.

DON'T GET too CLOSE, AND DON'T TRY to TOUCH It.

UNLESS YOU'RE A FLOWER, It SHOULD LOSE INTEREST AND FLY AWAY.

AND IF MORE PEOPLE LIKE YOU
GIVE BEES A CHANCE, THEY
MIGHT JUST HAVE, WELL... A CHANCE!

...to MAKE THE WORLD
A SWEETER PLACE.

For my parents: my favorite teachers; my biggest cheerleaders.
Thanks for all the unconditional love.
John Thomas Hogan, 1946–2014
Carol Jo Hogan, 1946–2014

Author's very important note: As an illustrator, I've taken some artistic license depicting the bees (mostly honeybees) in this book. Honeybees have 6 legs. Bethany-Barton-book bees appear to have only 2 legs . . . because drawing zillions of bee legs is boring. (Ha! Not really. It just looked messy.) Make sure to check out the endpapers for anatomically correct bees—complete with 6 legs!

PUFFIN BOOKS
An imprint of Penguin Random House LLC, New York

First published in the United States of America by Viking, an imprint of Penguin Random House LLC, 2017
Published by Puffin Books, an imprint of Penguin Random House LLC, 2019

Copyright © 2017 by Bethany Barton

Visit us online at penguinrandomhouse.com

LIBRARY OF CONGRESS CATALOGING-IN-PUBLICATION DATA IS AVAILABLE

Puffin Books ISBN 9780593113721

Manufactured in Spain

13

The artwork in this book was rendered using inks, paper, computers, Photoshop, laughter, iced tea, exhaustion, and silliness. Oh, and bees. Sort of.

HORNFACED Bee

(SOLITARY BEE WITH NO QUEEN WHO BUILDS ITS OWN PRIVATE NEST!)

YELLOW-FACED Bee

(INGESTS POLLEN INSTEAD OF COLLECTING IT WITH HAIRS LIKE OTHER BEES!)

CUCKOO Bee

(LAYS EGGS IN THE NESTS OF OTHER BEES, SO ITS LARVAE CAN STEAL THEIR FOOD!)

METALLIC GREEN BEE

(OFTEN BUILDS ITS SEPARATE NEST CLOSE TO OTHERS, SOMETIMES SHARING AN ENTRANCE...; LIKE BEE-APARTMENTS!)

EASTERN CARPENTER BEE

(BORES HOLES INTO WOOD TO LAY EGGS AND NEST!)

LEAF-CUTTER BEE

(CUTS PIECES OF LEAVES WITH ITS JAW TO LINE ITS NEST!)